Lennox Berkeley

Sonatine
for clarinet and piano
1928

Chester Music

SONATINE

CLARINET in A

I

LENNOX BERKELEY

Moderato
dolce e tranquillo

Appassionato
Pno.

V.S.

Clarinet in A

76

_p_

82

88

poco rit.

92 **A tempo**

dolce

_p_

98

104

Pno.

6

115

_f_ —————— _p_

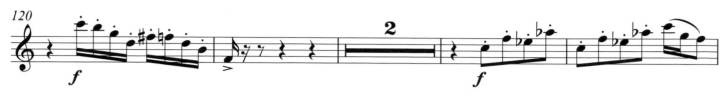

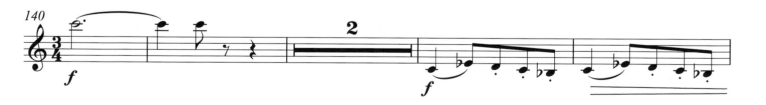

II

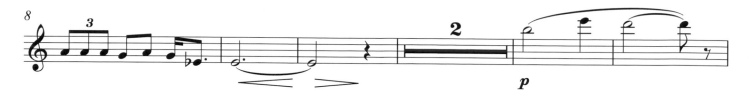

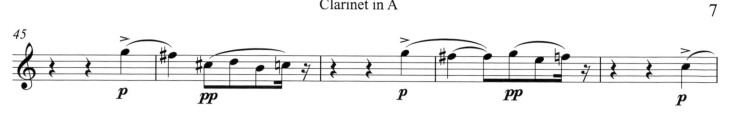

III

(Time)

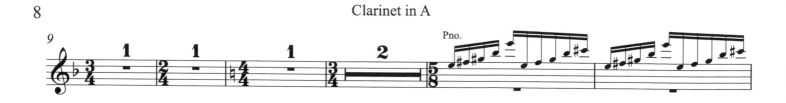

Lennox Berkeley

Sonatine
for clarinet and piano
1928

Chester Music

SONATINE

I

CLARINET in B♭

LENNOX BERKELEY

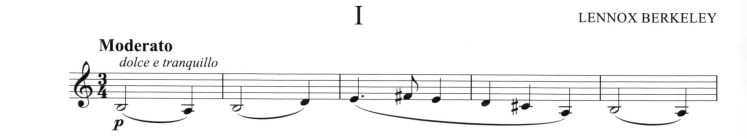

Appassionato

Pno.

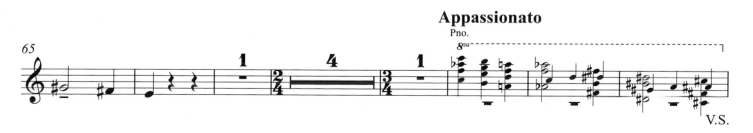

V.S.

A tempo
dolce

Pno.

6

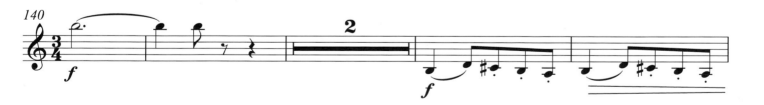

II

III

(Time)

Clarinet in B♭